Poetic Pets

Iris Carden

A catalogue record for this book is available from the National Library of Australia

For everyone who has ever loved a pet.

Princess

Collar bell jingles, soft paw pats her ball,
Princess is playing her way down the hall.

She wiggles her bum as she targets a pounce,
knocks things off the shelf to see if they bounce.

She leaps into a lap for a moment or two,
but can't stay there when there's so much to do.

The world is all new, there's so much to explore,
for this little kitten there's adventures galore!

She scampers and climbs, she runs then she stays,
Life is a game, won't you please come and play?

Then all of a sudden, she comes to a stop,
She gives a small yawn, and she falls with a flop.

And then with a deep self-satisfied purr
she forms a tight ball of warm snuggly fur.

She twitches a whisker and breathes long and deep
the sweet gentle snore of an innocent sleep.

Mr Bumpy is Human

Today I'll be a human, because that's what I choose.
I'll start my day with coffee, and I'll watch the TV news.

I won't go to the garden to just to lie out in the sun,
and I won't go climbing tress, even though it's lots of fun.

I will act like I'm in charge and tell pets what they should do,
I will eat just what I feel like, but I'll ration what's for you.

Why do you clean the kitchen? What's this thing called "work"?
I thought that being human would have a few more perks.

You wouldn't have to wash your clothes if you could just lick fur.
Instead of doing dishes, why not have a nap and purr?

The litter tray is smelly. Someone else can deal with that.
I've stopped being human 'cause I'd rather be a cat.

When you've finished with the litter, you can refill my bowl.
I'll be out there in the garden, having a little stroll.

And when the sunlight makes me sleepy, I'll know what to do,
because a cat always has time, and is free to have a snooze.

Fanta

Fanta smiles a huge doggy grin.
Her tongue hangs out below her chin.

With a glint in her eye and a fold in her ear
She loves to have her humans near.

She's chubbier than a dog should be,
But lives her life with endless glee.

Brown and cream and shades in-between.
Boisterous, and bouncy, but never mean.

Strong tail whips back and forth at speed,
and knocks things over with no heed.

She lifts her eyebrows as she listens.
Licks her black nose to make it glisten.

Doofy and dumb and endless fun,
Throw her a toy and watch her run.

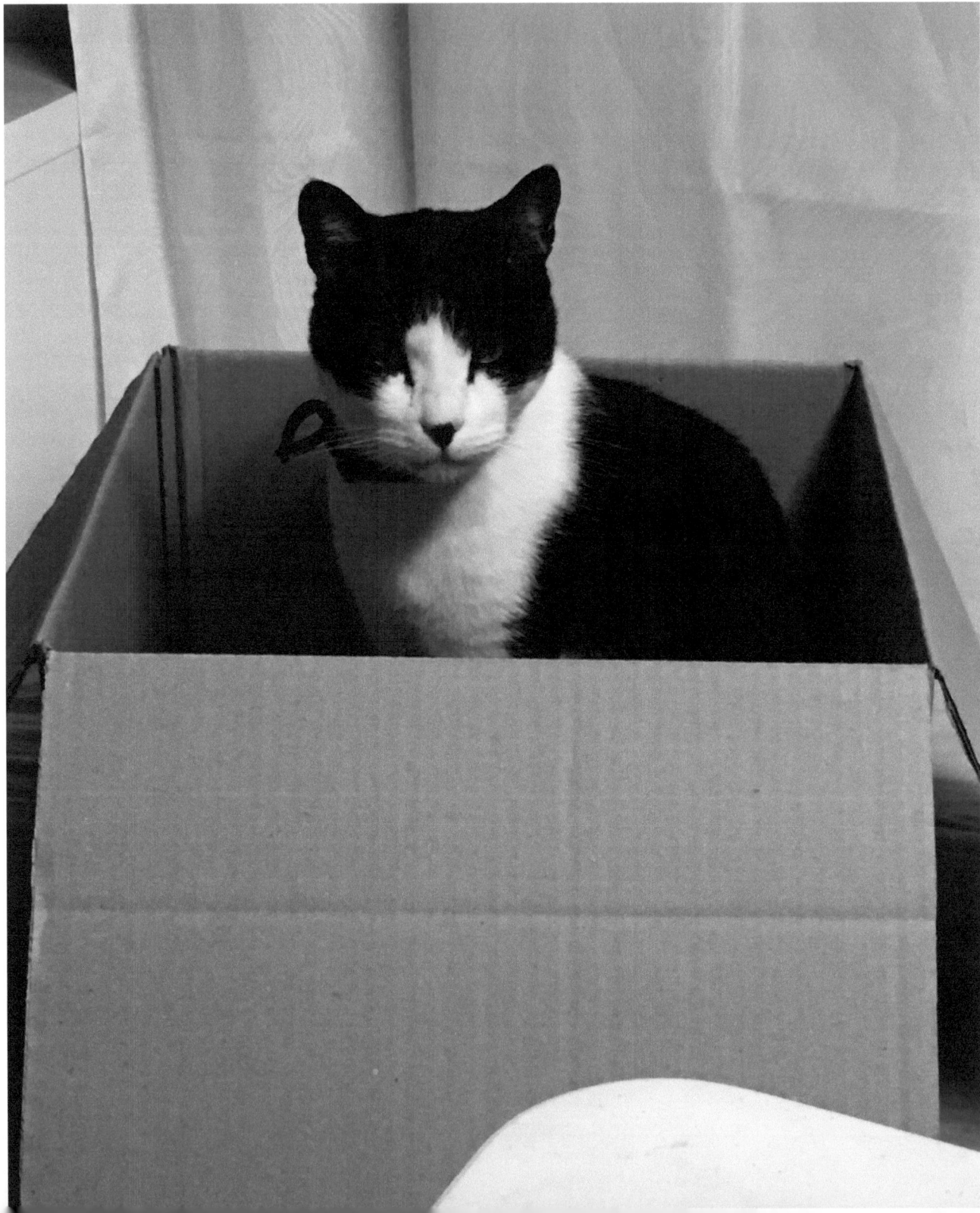

They Seek Him Here

They seek him here.
They seek him there.
Those humans
seek him everywhere.

Is he inside?
Is he outside?
That sneaky cat
knows how to hide!

Santa, Please

Santa please remember
I try so hard to be good.
I try to do all of the things
a real good doggy would.

I try not to bark at neighbours
and not to empty the bin,
but temptation often calls,
and I sometimes give in.

I really cannot tell you
what makes pillows explode.
Strange things just seem to happen,
when no-one is at home.

When the humans have gone out,
and I'm here all alone,
I may search all through the garbage
and hope to find a bone.

When my humans all are here,
I'm loving and I'm sweet.
A cute, and charming doggy,
who must deserve a treat.

So Santa Claws this Christmas
remember, oh will you please,
I'm really such a good doggy,
(when anybody sees.)

Belly Rubs

Come and rub a kitten belly.
You know that you want to.
I've been here just waiting,
for belly rubs from you.

When you tickle this little tum,
I'll pretend to scratch your hand,
but please tickle it anyway.
It's a game, you understand.

I'm a happy purring kitten,
and you can be happy too.
Rub my little fluffy tummy,
and you really can't feel blue.

Three Pets in a Bed

There were three in the bed
and all of them said,
"No room for a human.
Sleep elsewhere instead."

The human said, "Wait!
It's my bed you're in.
Surely there's room.
Some of you are quite thin."

The pets wouldn't move.
They just wouldn't share.
The human said, "It's my bed.
I'm sleeping in there."

Then the human, quite
unceremoniously,
picked up all the pets
one, two and three.

She put all of them
out of the room with care,
then closed the door
and left them all there.

You know the above is all a lie.
In truth, she made the decision
to fit carefully between pets
and sleep in an awkward position.

Kitten to Cat

Once you had a little kitten
she was cute and soft and small.
She slept in a kitten basket,
and played with her little ball.

But something happened to her
as months and months went by.
Your kitten grew much larger,
and her markings more defined.

And now it is so obvious.
You really should know that:
where you used to have a kitten,
now you have a cat.

She plays and sleeps and acts the same.
It's really no surprise.
Your cat is just a kitten
of a somewhat greater size.

Cat, Assembly Required

Don't buy a cat from Ikea.
The instructions are never quite clear.
You add this to that,
and instead of a cat,
It's the modern art work of the year!

Let Sleeping Dogs Lie

Go away I'm asleep,
I'm not getting up.
The night was too short,
for this oversized pup.

I'm staying in bed
whatever you say.
I'm sleeping in
for all of the day.

What did you say?
It's time for a walk?
Well that's different.
OK, let's talk.

If there's one thing
I love more than sleep,
it's go go for a walk
right down our street.

When the other dogs bark
as they see me walk by,
because they're shut in
and I'm right outside.

Property of Bumpy

This is my human.
I won't share with you.
I'll fight if you dare
snuggle up to him, too.

I'm happy to share
the other humans you see.
But this special one
belongs only to me.

I claimed him
a very long time ago.
I've comforted him,
and I've watched him grow.

So he is my human,
and mine alone,
You must be aware
if you come to my home.

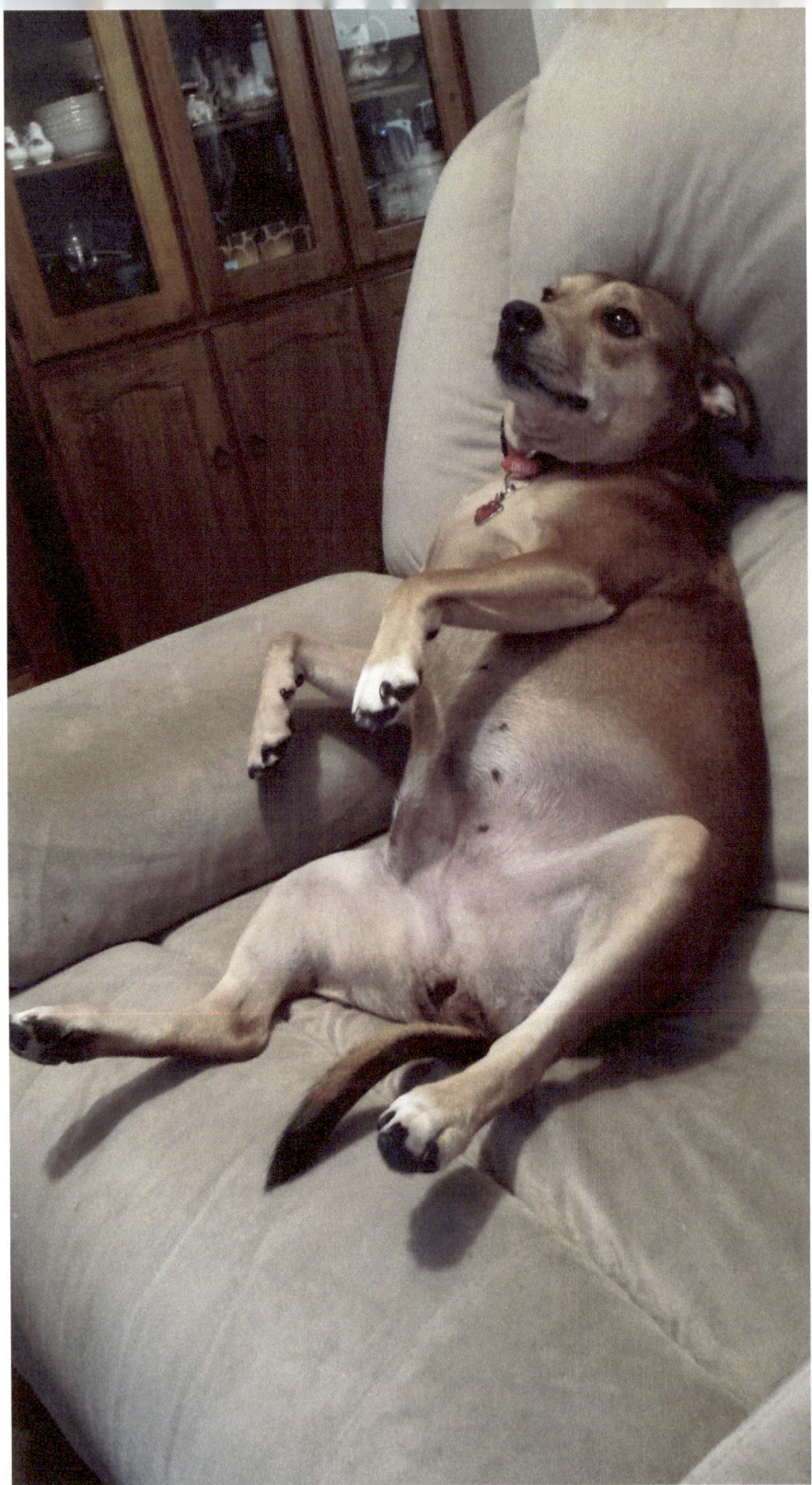

A Dog's Life

I'm living a dog's life.
There's time to rest and think.
I don't have to work for food
or for water to drink.

A philosophical dog
contemplating things,
like why the sky is up,
and why a birdie sings.

And why do certain cats
think they rule the world?
And how hard it is for me
to be such a good girl?

It's a great thing for a dog
just to be so free,
to just lie back and think
so philosophically.

Best Friends

When the humans have all go out
and you feel all alone,
that's when you need a best friend
to call your very own.

A friend who wants to play your games,
or just rest by your side,
or helps you get in mischief,
and the evidence to hide.

When the humans come back home
we'll be rivals once again,
we'll compete for their attention,
and we'll hide that we're best friends.

Flop Cat

Kittens love to play and run
but then they come to a stop.
The switch seems to turn off .
The kitten just goes flop.

Kittens only have too speeds
two settings on the cat.
They are either going full flat out
or they fall out flat.

King of the House

I'm the king of the house
all fall down before me.
I'm in charge of everything
and the humans all adore me.

I deserve the very best,
Of everything I need.
I'm the cat who rules the rest.
All of my demands you'll heed.

Today I only run the house
iron fist in velvet paw.
But tomorrow I will be the boss
when I rule the whole wide world.

More about the pets in this book at www.mrbumpycat.com

More by this author at www.lulu.com/spotlight/IrisCarden

www.ingramcontent.com/pod-product-compliance
Lightning Source LLC
Chambersburg PA
CBHW042012080426
42734CB00002B/54